Sing for the Taxman

To John and Ella Whitehead

Sheenagh Pugh

Sing for the Taxman

SEREN BOOKS

SEREN BOOKS is the book imprint of
Poetry Wales Press Ltd.
Andmar House, Tondu Road
Bridgend, Mid Glamorgan
CF31 4LJ

British Library Cataloguing in Publication Data:

Pugh, Sheenagh
Sing For The Taxman
I. Title
821.914

ISBN: 1-85411-085-3

The publisher acknowledges the financial support of the Welsh Arts Council

Cover Art: Giovanni d' Andrea: 'Lira da braccio', 1511, (it's ivory label reads 'Song is doctor to the pain of man'), reproduced courtesy of the Kunsthistorisches Museum, Vienna, Austria

CONTENTS

Climbing Hermaness

Burrafirth

Turn left at the northernmost
village, and just go west
until west runs out. The road
ends with Burrafirth.

At the end of all things
there is a flower meadow,
a great meadow enamelled
with rose-root and red fescue,
a meadow of eyebright,
moonwort and tormentil,
a meadow of black cattle
wading through sunlight
and the scent of thyme; a meadow
with a salt edge, bright colours
blurring into shingle,
a meadow between two shoulders,
huge and green, hunched each side
along the glittering firth:
Saxa Vord and Hermaness,
shrugging at the Atlantic.

There is a great longing
to go no further, to be
beguiled, like the voyagers
of legend. *Why go west,*
the sweet whisper runs, *ahead*
are dragons, and someone leaves
the quest, to wander for ever
in the meadow of heart's ease.

But most go on,
shouldering their gear, looking
back at the jewelled grass,
because beyond the west
there is still a way westward,
because there is Hermaness
to climb: the last cliff
on the last island.

And they start upward, watched
by the incurious cattle
on the beach, munching blue gentians
that taste of salt.

Hermaness

The path is not, at first,
steep; more like a stroll
in the sun. When we look down,
the dust seems to glint: a child,
entranced, squats, pouring it
over his hair in handfuls.
The parents groan, but he rises,
holding both hands up, clean,
and glittering... There are gasps,
then explanations: gneiss,
silica, serpentine; guidebook words
put things in their place. Ahead,
the child with the sparkling hair
touches a silvered finger
to his mouth, tasting the wonder.

The mountain sounds
with life: little peat-burns
mutter underfoot, ribboning
the rock; grasshoppers whirr

like power-lines. The path
is mined with rabbit-holes
and black moths that start
out of the heather. Or a patch
of ground opens its eyes; gazes
gravely up, while the mother
circles overhead.

The climb so slow,
it is a small shock
to look down at black dots
browsing in the meadow.
There is mist ahead,
where the mountain curves up
into a steep green wall.
Across the firth, the crest
of Saxa Vord is drowned
in whiteness; now and then,
when it swirls back, great domes
and towers appear briefly
and bright: the caliph's palace
of the air force, listening
from their outpost, scanning
the ocean for enemies.

It is a hut
on the edge of sight
we have to make for,
a smudge on the green slope.
Sometimes the path, or the mist,
dips, and it isn't there:
when it comes back, it never
seems any nearer.

In the dips are patches
of bright treacherous green,

that give underfoot,
sucking. The path stumbles
between heather-clumps; sometimes
an old plank wobbles
across quagmire. Either side
is the pale fluff of bog-cotton;
the sundew, that feeds
on flies; the spotted orchids,
just out of reach. *And do not,*
on your quest, go aside
from the path : all adventurers
get warned about that.

So long looking down,
picking the way: when at last
the ground firms, it is like freedom
to see the firth, the shining
sleeve, pleated with ripples.
Look back: the meadow
is long gone, closed off
behind cliffs, their crevices
lit with sea-pink and the white
of kittiwakes.

The climb to the hut
is steep now; no path trodden,
too few come so far. The safe way
is marked with posts; you fix
the next in your eye: *I'll make it*
that far. The pure air rasps
in the throat; all adventurers
lean on that wall, as if
there were nothing left
to take them on,

till someone says: *right,*
that's the climb done,
just a bit further north
and we'll be there.

Muckle Flugga

The marshland is left
behind, and the brown peat-burns.
We are higher here than snipe
or pipit; higher than butterwort
and yellow asphodel; higher than water,
except the fine salt spray
that hangs in the air.
Colours are colder: squill,
small and blue, like a haze
above the grass. Up here,
the fiddle-scrape of crickets
dies in the level note
of the wind. Even the clamour
from the raucous gannet ledges
drifts up muted.

There is a coldness
of mist, sun-pierced; it swirls
below us, blanking out
the world. Somewhere down there
is the great sheet of brilliance,
the northern ocean, and the rock
of the last lighthouse.
It is not in the tale
that the adventurers come
so far, and cannot see it;
yet it could be. The chill
settles about: there is no reward
for climbing; mountains owe nothing.

But it does clear,
briefly; in a swift moment
it scrolls back, and our eyes search
the blinding brightness for the black
of Muckle Flugga. And we see,
just for an instant, the tower
gleaming through rags of mist.
And beyond the last lighthouse
is the last rock,
the Out Stack, and beyond that
the resplendent sea. And when
the mist pours back, it is almost
welcome, in that place
of ultimates with no end
but light itself.

The old voyagers
would have set sail, hearts thudding,
for the edge, but we know
there are no edges.
We have outclimbed water and land;
we have come to this place
which is sky-coloured flowers
and salty grass; which is wind
aching in the ears; which is light
locked above whiteness,
and there is no insight, no knowledge
to take back; not the flowers,
nor the rare minerals, nor the black moths.
What lives here is for itself:
it must stay, when we go down
the only way we can.

Magnus

I saw him in a bar last night: beer in,
wit out, his loud mouth declaiming
slow, angry nonsense. A smaller man
helped him away, swaying, carrying
twelve cans of Tennents in a plastic bag,
and the others laughed and said: that's Magnus.

And he fell out into the blue midnight
of the north: Magnus king of Norway,
Magnus the earl, his white skull axe-split
into sainthood... Down in Lerwick today,
a little crowd was watching him be sick
by the harbour: he'd had the cans for breakfast.

In the Sound, some klondyker leaks
oil, by the look of it, long tarnished ribbons
at the tide's edge. Magnus has the shakes
from the cloying smell. He leans on the stanchions
staring, not seeing the glittering path
of light. He might be a husband, a father.

He shows me the worst: I must surmise the best,
Magnus with his blood's tide running clear,
deft fingers unlocked from his fist,
eyes swept of cobwebs, seeing sharp and far
as a sea-king's; good words tasting sweet
in his mouth: whole, holy: Magnus the great.

Fogbound

Baltasound was shrinking. Fog sucked up
the hills: Muckle Heog, Nikka Vord
took their leave. Quite near, the tiny airstrip
paused on the edge of sight.

Surfaces were muffled; no light bounced
off the Sound's dulled mirror. You could have wrung
the grey sky out like a sponge. They jumped off
the plane, new-landed from Aberdeen,
their faces fever-bright, the men
who wouldn't make Chevron's rig that night.

The hotel bar was packed to the blind windows;
they were radiant, high, couldn't stop talking
or let the night end. Nobody mentioned
licensing hours. They were still fired up
when I crawled off to bed.

I peered out
next morning, about six. The blue sky
looked washed clean; sunlight glinted metallic
off the water. They were boarding a little bus
for the airstrip, shoulders sagging
in surrender; slate-faced, ash-mouthed,
the light sucked out of them.

Polar Bearings

An airport with a couple of runways,
a small terminal, and a white bear.

He was spotted by a baggage-handler
last month, glimmering on the rim
of arctic dark: baggage-handlers go
about their work in twos, these days.

In the transit lounge, people chat about him,
offhand, glancing out of window
once in a while. Pilots take off
for the safety of meteor-showers; unwind
to the radio-static of ice-hail, flying blind
and relaxed over the Barents Sea.

Touching down again with a nervous laugh,
they hobnob with scientists, oilmen, a sightseer
or two. There's no such thing as a stranger
any more: they're all in the same story
in the airport on the edge of light,

seeing further, hearing a footfall,
hearts racing, living at the limit,
tasting the cold, the coffee, their own fears.

And when the fog sweeps in; piles in a drift
against the windows, there's a communal
intake of breath. Who's to say, when it clears,
there won't be a patch of white left?

Sing For The Taxman

If that's a sea of faces,
the wind is your voice,
patterning them with light,
singing up a storm
night after night.

What takes you out there still,
and you an old man? When you wake
on the tour bus, stiff, your back aching,
and home doesn't call, and all you feel
is a longing to draw the tides again
in the next town: what sort of man?

Fifty-eight, looking ten years older,
ten good years, and what's to do
but to get your band together and go

on the road again, while the road's still there,
while there's still somewhere you haven't been?
And they say you're singing for the taxman,

that a decade's dues slipped your mind,
so he's letting you tour to raise the wind.
And it could be; yet who, hearing,

could ever suppose you had a choice;
or could do anything but sing,
as long as the words were there, and your voice?

Iron hair tied back, Indian-fashion
in a headband from the crag face,
black eyes in grey rock, thinking
pain into music.

It was no otherwise
with old Egil, staring out
at his son's killer, the sword
idle at his side: *how can I fight*
the sea?

It moved in him: loss
and sorrow, their tides tugging
his feet, battering away
at the brittle sandstone.
What am I but rock,
numbed and senseless,
written on by weather,
rain-pocked, salt-eaten ...

And the words flashed in the air
like sun off metal, like pure joy
of craft, as they settled
into his pattern.

He was a fighter, a hired sword,
loud drunk and angry silent,
sharp-tongued to kings, dumbstruck
with a woman. You and the boys
would have loved him: he was Pancho,
all the outlaws, the stranger from Blue Rock,
the highwayman come back.

And he could write it: oh yes,
somewhere behind the black brows
it all boiled down
to the bones: the shape of a battle,
a friend set in the wrought silver

of praise; the aching space
where a son was.

Once, too, he sang for the taxman;
ransomed his head from a king
with a cold catalogue
of kennings: *take your pick , Eirik,*
we both know I didn't mean
a single glittering phrase, but Christ,
can't I craft them, just!

Many men on Vin Moor
heard the curious hiss
of arrows; saw blood ribboning
through the river, iron flaming blue
in a man's hand: only one
knew the words for it.

The words for hurting; for missing
a friend, or wanting a woman;
for hating or being happy.

It was a language he spoke;
it came natural, as music
comes to you. I've seen you on stage,
shaping some thought as a guitar chord,
a pause, a slight catch in a word;
translating into the fluent rasp-edge
of your voice.

This is the language
that few speak, and all recognise:
that happened to me; that's just how it is...
that's the way I'd say it, if I could.

Egil rocking his grief
in the dark; taking no food,
being nagged to live: *why,*
with Bodvar drowned?
And his daughter, snapping back:
"my brother needs
a song, and who else
knows the words for it?"

What was I given
that had to be paid
with such a tax?
What but the gift
to grieve aloud; to hold him
in words; to put shape
on my thanks, and my hate?

Sing for the outlaws: sing for the man dead
on Christmas morning; for the kiss of Pride
that killed prejudice; for the Cherokee
in your blood, and the time-stranded cowboy
in your heart. Sing for the whiskey river
and the weed high; for the old Martin guitar
you loved so much and wore a hole in,
and it still played sweet: sing for the long pain
in your back; for whatever makes pain speak,
whatever makes grief delight in music.
Sing because you're the best; because you can,
and sing — why not?— for the taxman.

Small Change

The train I'm on is well late already,
crawling behind a slow local freight,
with an endless scrapyard filling the window.
It looks like rain. I can't make out the spelling
on these poems; I fear my student is not
Blake come back. There's no call, no movement
of eagles; no words on fire. They're all
like that, my class: taking pains, uninspired.

There's nowhere I have to be, as it happens,
so the delay's no matter; it gives me
time for a closer look. This phrase moves better
than some; this image works more or less
as it should. Outside, a steering-wheel slowly rocks
silver in the dodgy light, perched on a pile
of cars whose bruises shimmer; rust touched
with violet.

Something small and grey skims over
the yard. It does not take the breath away
with beauty; it is no high, falling death,
like a hawk. Its flight is low: yet it does fly,
and a spadeful of the earth is in its shadow.

Headsound

This train is full of music, rocking
off the beat, echoing all over
the coach; yet folk are just talking
or reading. I never did this before,
and I can't believe sound's not leaking

out of these earphones. Everyone sits so quiet,
while it's floodtide in my head, the honey
and the rasp, blending: *"take it to the limit"*,
their two voices part, soar, seamlessly
reunite. It's true: no-one can hear it

outside my wires' circle; it's just Waylon,
Willie and me in here. I show the guard
my ticket; smile, feeling like an island.
Beyond the waves, a child chants one word
over and over. There's a sharp suit dialling

on a mobile phone; the man behind the *Mirror*
eyes him briefly. Perhaps, if I switched off,
I'd hear from each the faint, tinny stridor
of his own private music, the inner life
that surges so in the ears of its one hearer.

Mozart Playing Billiards

Wolfie drifting round the table
so casual; he had a rhythm,
you know, that cue was part of his arm.
I don't suppose he was even in here
that often, but he was the kind they all
watch: such a sweet mover.

He could have been great: I told him so,
only his heart was never in it.
Playing just relaxed him; helped him write.
You'd see him cock an ear to the click
of the balls; then he'd grab a cue
and tap out tunes, for God's sake.

Catchy tunes, too; folk hummed them
all round town: he had class, Wolfie,
whatever he did... Well, I tell a lie,
there was one thing. That man,
I swear, had the foulest mouth on him.
I'd have to insist, every so often,

please, Wolfie, less of the effing.
Odd, isn't it? Give him a harpsichord
or a cue, he was magic; yet every word
was an embarrassment. Well, there you are,
a man can't be good at everything.
... God, though, he could have been a player.

Duet In Central Park

There are two men, and one is a genius,
a poet, a composer. The other has a sweet voice.

The one has a way of putting sorrow
and wit in words, so that you feel they came from you.

Then he fits the text to the note so fine,
you'd think no other music could ever be in

those words: it's so perfect, a man could cry.
Yet if you hummed the tunes; read the poetry

to yourself, you wouldn't feel it; nor would you if
the poet, the composer, alone sang his grief.

That's what the man beside him is about,
the man in whose head is neither word nor note

of his own: whose voice is the translation,
clear and accurate, of what is written down.

He understands that which he cannot do,
missing no subtle grace-note; giving each word its due,

while, somewhere under the carrying melodies,
the poet's small voice helps out with the close-harmonies.

Book

I am the thought that flies in seconds
through a man's head, and lives for ever.

I am all he knew: I am his words
on the other side of the world,
sounding long after he dies.

I can cure the sick; build bridges,
change your mind, choke you with tears.
I can make a world, and man it.

Give me to a child, I am the ocean
cupped in his hands: I am all the sand
of the beach in his toy bucket.
I am the key to the walled garden,
the magic lamp, the island
where the treasure is.

I am could-be and might-have-been,
the story of the people, the store
of seed-corn. I feed the hunger
that grain leaves keen.

Two Miles

Hello. I will just give the baby
to my mother-in-law; then we can talk
while I feed the pigs. Yes, I know,
you are the stranger building the sea dyke,
to make new land for rice. My eldest son
is helping on it.

We miss him in our fields, of course,
but we do not mind the extra work,
because it will be worth it. We have an acre
or so: we grow groundnuts, a few roots,
but mainly rice. We can grow about half
of what we need.

Yes, I have lived all my life
in Phuong Nam. We are twelve here,
what with me and my husband and our mother,
and the children, and my son's wife
and baby. I beg your pardon? No,
I have never seen the sea.

It is two miles off; that is a long walk,
and I am busy here, or in the fields,
as long as light lasts. Besides, the sea
is no use, unless you are a fisherman.
My son fishes, sometimes. And once he brought
a shell back, with the sea's sound

trapped in it. You look wondering: I expect
the language is hard for you. I must go back
to the fields now. The old lady will talk
to you: at her age, there is more time.
I am looking forward to the new land:
we can grow double the rice.

The Last Wolf In Scotland

I am a wolf. I know this
from way back, when my mother's
hot tongue prickled over the heap
that was me and the others,
as she whispered: *wolf wolf wolf wolf.*

There are four kinds: wolf,
not-wolf, wolf-food and hurt-wolf.
Not-wolf does nothing to the world:
wolf-food is warm, floods your throat,
fills your guts with sleep. Hurt-wolf
stiffens hairs, sharpens eyes and ears,
thumps inside you.

Wolf smelled different
from the world. When I was blind,
all the dark smelled of wolf: later
we blinked our way into a dazzle
of smells: a music, note overlaying
note, but always the deep one
under all.

The other day
I went to drink, and wolf
looked up at me. I'd forgotten
the face. So long since I touched
wolf. I used to find
tracks sometimes, or fancy I heard
a call at full moon. Never near.

I miss that smell, the gap
in the pattern, the note I can't hear
in the music. I miss fur and tongues
and singing voices. I miss the piece
that fell out of the world.

Palestinian

He lies in a scrolled ball,
leaving room to pass
on the pavement.

His head nods over the kerb,
bleeding tidily
into the gutter.

Such reticence, such neatness
don't suit a young man.
Get up, my dear: take up space,

shout, as you should, as you did,
before your knees were clasped
to your chest,

like a child's shadow
on an ultrascan; before
the heavy poppy head

on the bruised weak neck
nodded over; spilled its petals
in a red splash.

After You

I stand aside when I see old ladies
in bus queues, for fear of being flattened.
Some are all elbows and umbrellas;
some little round balls

that bounce off you, unhurt, and mount
the steps while you count your bruises.
They bemoan the decline of manners in fierce
squeaky voices like Mighty Mouse.

Back twenty years, when I was young,
I'd have given them a mouthful, no bother;
now I just feel like patting their heads,
and it's hard to keep pity out

of my face. I suppose I see them
beating me to the last seat
on Charon's ferry: after you, by all means,
I'm in no hurry.

The Turkish Policeman's Testimony

"He hit his head against the wall,
your honour, and committed suicide."

Raising of grave judicial eyebrows:
smothered titters from smartass reporters.
The policeman's face is open, without guile.

"No, that's how it was. Listen,
we'd been at it all night; I'd ask him
how long he'd been a terrorist; which friends
were in the Party.

He asked me
why I grilled people; didn't it upset me?

I said I had my job to do. I asked him
why he made trouble; read forbidden books.

He said, because they were there. He asked
if I ever questioned my orders, or wondered
if my bosses were wrong.

I told him I'd never get any work done
like that. He said it was like talking
to the wall. We tried different languages,
still no good. I couldn't interpret
his silence; he couldn't figure out
my hand signs, even when I wrote them
in his face. In the end, by beating
his head repeatedly against the wall,
he killed himself, your honour: people do,
when they're frustrated."

Jenny

The beach curved, white and wide, out
beyond the cliff, until there was a place
where land, sea, sky all looked as if they met,
dissolving, dazzling. I was half-asleep,
while the sea shifted, and the land changed shape,
and all the edges smudged in the sun's haze.

She looms up, blotting out a mountain
with her flowered dress; the note of surf
dies in her complaints: *have you seen*
a little girl in yellow, about four,
Jenny her name is; been gone half an hour
and her mother's frantic ... Her voice ebbs off

in hopelessness before I say no,
and she plods on, and I take a look
through the field-glasses now, searching out yellow
at the sucking tide's edge. I let them sweep
the dunes where a man might lurk: once they pick up
Jenny's gran, slow and sad, walking back.

I see each flower, and, where her permed white hair
has thinned, the pink skin's mortality,
and the whole bright profound arc of air
is altered by her, the sleeve of sea unravelled,
the beach crowded with laughing shadows, a world
without a strand of sense, empty of Jenny.

The Slow Fall

It was the first frost of October,
the first morning with enough chill
to chip the leaves. They wrinkled the canal
like a golden skin; you could see no water,

and the black barge came on, slowly,
scissoring the cloth with its bow,
but in its wake was still seamless yellow,
as if nothing had ever been by,

and the stave's bright notes fell through the sun
like ash or dust. One glittering coin lit
on the steersman's hand: he smiled and waved it
in passing, at the still, grave fishermen.

FIVE VOICES

Johann Joachim Quantz, flautist

I met the late Lieutenant quite often
in the Prince's rooms. I should explain
that the King's Majesty never approved
of his son learning the flute. Lieutenant Katte
used to keep watch, and give us good warning
of his approach. It didn't always work:
I remember one time, he leaned
round the door: "The ogre's coming
on the run. I'd lose that fancy gown,
if I were you." This was an over-robe
the Prince had on; he threw it in a corner,
and we all started stuffing sheet music
down the backs of sofas. The Lieutenant
couldn't stop laughing: I felt sick
with panic. He gestured at my coat:
"You know red puts him in a bad mood?"
We could hear the King's voice now, bellowing
along the corridor, and the Prince
was chalk-white: "Katte, he'll smash the flutes."
The Lieutenant clapped him on the shoulder,
(I could never get used to his lack
of formality, his casual manners).
"It's all right, we'll hide 'em." He grinned
at me, and opened the big wood-cupboard
— half-empty, thank God. I huddled with him
in the stuffy, resinous dark, door held shut,
listening to the bedlam. Mostly shouts
or thuds, as the King fetched some book a kick;
once there was a great crackling sound
and an odd smell. The Lieutenant nudged me
and whispered: "He's pitched the dressing-gown
on the fire." His eyes gleamed: I swear

he enjoyed the danger. I was rigid,
my palms hurting where the nails dug in,
if only he doesn't look in here.
Catch me in a red coat again,
or passing the time of day with princes
and mad officers who can't stifle
inapt mirth... He was still convulsed;
my hand itched to hold his mouth shut
(is that etiquette, in a wood-cupboard?).
It seemed an age before the door slammed
behind the King, and we stumbled out.
I had cramp in both feet: he was still laughing,
until he saw blood on the Prince's mouth.
That sobered him cold enough; his face froze
like a hard winter. Myself, I took my flute
and my departure. I'd had enough
of the quality. If I think of him now,
he's always laughing in the dark.

Peter Keith, ex-Prussian Army officer

Damn beer's flat. A man might as well
be in the army. God, I don't miss that.
I never had any dreams of glory,
but in Prussia, a man had no choice;
the whole bloody country was a barracks.
I was born to it too, but... I don't know,
my people weren't native Prussian, you see;
just Scottish adventurers who fetched up
in foreign parts. I've never felt at home
anywhere, so the idea of exile
didn't worry me, not that I ever thought
it would come to that. Well, would *you* credit
a crown prince who planned to skip the country?

Oh, he had good cause, no question.
I was his best friend, bar his sister
and Katte; and not a day went by
that he wasn't shouted at in public,
kicked round the carpet, mocked, whatever
took the old goat's fancy. I'd not have stayed
at home for that, but then my father
wasn't the king. *Nobody* walks out
on a kingdom. When he asked me and Katte
to plan it for him, I really thought
it was just a dream; it'd keep his spirits up
maybe, but come the day, he'd think again.
I didn't do much: arranged a few horses.
It was Katte, with his class, his gift
of the gab, who spoke to the embassies,
squared the French. And I never thought
he meant it, either. I mean to say,
he *was* army, a field-marshal's grandson,
for all his books and music. Besides which,
he never sounded serious about anything

for long. I've heard him spend half an hour
proving God didn't exist; he'd have talked
the Pope round. So I asked: since when
was he an atheist, and he grinned: "Since
it got fashionable."

It was one day
I went to his rooms: I think, to borrow money,
and I stopped outside because I could hear
a woman: aha, the usual, I thought,
but it wasn't. This was a lady, speaking French,
arguing with him, and I knew the voice.
"It will never work; you must talk Friedrich
out of it" — and it came to me then,
it was the princess. She was very angry;
Katte was trying to laugh it off,
and they say she was sweet on him, you know:
"If you think a prince's friend walks safe,
you're wrong." And then him, stung for once:
"If I die, it will be in a good cause."

Die? I damn near did. I sat on the step.
God, he's right, we could; it's desertion,
treason, what have you... My mind was whirling;
it was happening, the fools were going through
with it, and I wanted out. *She* knew;
who else? The old bastard had spies
all over the household. Good cause bedamned:
if I die, there'll be nothing good about it.
I'd have run that night, but I was too scared
to make my mind up. I hung around
a few days, biting my nails, till someone
tipped us the wink that it was all up,
and I rode straight for the border.

Why Katte didn't,
I can't think; maybe there was some girl
he had to say goodbye to, or maybe
dying in his good cause appealed to him.
He did it well, from what I heard. Here's to him.
This beer isn't as bad as I thought:
I must be getting used to it.

Georg Lisiewsky, portrait painter

I know that head. I've had the brow
in my calipers, I know its exact span.
I know how the eyelids half-close
in mockery. I know which colours to mix
for the pale tint of the hair: I know
just how much to darken it for the lashes.
There's a grin that starts at one corner
of the mouth, and when he speaks,
the head tilts slightly back on the neck.

On the neck... dear God, how long
are they going to leave it there uncovered?
I have never seen anything so wrong
as that head lying alone, apart
from the slumped body, arms flung out
at odd angles, and nothing as it should be.
I couldn't get the arms right: three times
I painted them over, and the natural line
still wouldn't flow, under that uniform.
It worried me: him too. I recall
our first sitting: "I want it done soon,
and done right." He was easy-going
in most ways, but he said that
in dead earnest. I wondered why
so urgent, such a young man as he was,
with all the time in the world.

The day I told him
I had the face finished, he came round
and looked a long, long time. He nodded
in the end: "Yes, it's good, it's like."
That was praise, from him, though he seemed
quiet rather than pleased. He stood still,
just looking. "I'll be young a long time,
thanks to you. But the arms are still wrong."

It was next day, out shopping
in town, I heard he'd been arrested.
Treason, desertion, I don't know. I thought
what'll happen to him , and then
if he dies, who'll buy the picture ?
I followed the trial, the sentence, waiting
for a reprieve. One day, I heard
two officers talking: "He was warned, you know,
the day of the arrest; he should have been
long gone, but the fool hung around."
"Some girl, was it?"

I nearly said: "no,
he just wanted to see the arms put right."
But I don't know that. And now they come
with a cloak, a deep splash of blue,
and drop it over the awkward wreck
of limbs, over the fair hair tied back,
and I'm not the man with the skill
to put him right now.

Colonel Reichmann, commanding at Küstrin Gaol

I beg to report that the execution
of Freiherr Hans Hermann von Katte,
formerly lieutenant, was carried out
yesterday, November sixth, according to orders,
at Küstrin. As His Majesty wished,
the Crown Prince witnessed the event
from his cell window. Indeed, as the prisoner
was escorted to the block, His Highness
called out to him: "Katte, pardonnez-moi."
The prisoner replied, also in French,
that there was no need, and that death
would be no trouble. He then walked on
with the guard, exchanging pleasantries
as if nothing were amiss. All witnesses
were moved by his demeanour. He was quite calm
throughout the execution, which proceeded
without a hitch.

As had been ordered,
the body was left, uncovered, for some hours
on view, before the family were permitted
to remove it. The prison guards inform me
that the Crown Prince fainted three times
in the course of the afternoon, and remains
in great distress. Everything has been done
exactly according to His Majesty's wishes.

Theodor Fontane, novelist

It was a chill day. We waited, huddled
and stamping, outside the big house,
while the servant hunted up the key.
He took us over the road, around the back
of the church, through long wet grass
to a small, squat, red-brick building.
There was nothing romantic about it,
no following a light down dark steps
into a crypt; he just unlocked the door
and there they were, the carved stone tombs,
cold and ornate. He pointed them out
to us: the general, the field-marshal,
knowing which one we'd come for.

You must look in the corner for the bad boy
in his plain wooden coffin. He has been
on his own ever since he came back,
by night, unannounced, without ceremony,
to be hushed up. Yet, ever since,
visitors have come calling on him
at the back of beyond. They take relics,
if they aren't watched: all the teeth
are gone, and the vertebra from his neck
that bore the sword-cut; some Englishman
made off with that, our guide told us
over his shoulder, keeping a sharp eye
on the white jumble of bones, the bright swathe
of hair still tied in its black ribbon.
I'd not have thought dead hair could gleam gold
like that: burnished armour, celandines
in March? I'll find a likeness later.

He was no great beauty, though. I've seen
his portrait, done the year he died.

A face neither handsome nor ugly;
witty; a little arrogant perhaps,
but very bright.

Lieutenant Hans Hermann von Katte,
born 28 February 1704; executed 6 November 1730.

Wust: Sachsen-Anhalt

Sandy pavements crumble
underfoot: between the cobbles
of the road, sand seeps. The shabby houses
are brown, rust, yellow, their edges
uncertain in the sun: a chunk
of sandstone gingerbread might break off
any moment, its dust glinting slowly
down. This place is going back to sand.

The old ladies in black
on their bikes have brittle bones
and small hopes. *For people our age,*
the train's long gone. They save scraps
for scrawny cats; shore up
the church tower fund, and stand
each morning at the baker's,
patient as fate.

A cock shrieks somewhere
into the stillness. Nettles grow
by the little mausoleum
where the beheaded soldier
lies easy, his teeth taken
for souvenirs. His hair was bright,
they say, like the sunflowers
in the allotment gardens.

The Man In The Mausoleum

Just over the road,
the pleasant manor
where he was at home,
where the horses knew
the ring of his step
on the stable yard.

There was a cup,
no doubt, and a chair,
that were known as his:
a room made ready
when he came on leave,
a place at table.

It takes a moment
to break a neck,
and suddenly a man
belongs elsewhere,
in a musty corner
of this dead house.

Over the road
dinner is served
with one place fewer;
horses are saddled
who would take fright
to see him now.

Servants run errands
over the road,
but no-one comes
with messages to him
from the house where, already,
he is a stranger.

Judas At Stendal

for Catherine Fisher

Stendal is a fine church: glass
like sunset, as far as I recall.
There was an altar, carved in stone lace
— or was that plaster? — and along the wall,

niches with statues: a bishop, a crusader,
apostles, angels; but the only one
who stays printed on my eye for ever
wore a leather noose: a dark wooden man,

whose mediaeval carver had made no mock
of him; teased no hooknose from the wood.
I can't forget the everyday look
on his face: the eyes not evil, just sad.

Remember, Remember

This slumped bag of rags in the barrow
isn't him: this sad clown's turniphead
not my tall soldier, my November hero,
my ruined sunlight. He has been dead

so long now: young, he fills my eyes,
but the children make him an old man
in their play; drag him begging for pennies
till fire twists his face, and he dies again.

I saw his face when he died the first time,
the thin paper with the bones' motif
traced through it. There was nothing of him:
he swayed on the scaffold like a leaf

in autumn. Now the day of thanksgiving
for his death blows the boys out of school,
scatters their laughter. And the birds are leaving;
the wind tosses them in a white handful.

at the heavy sky. Trees against the dark
burn: there's a young beech, leaves just kindled
gold at the edges, but the big oak
blazes yellow, and the rowan's red

crackles and glows. The old man who stands
in the wind's stream, letting the shreds of light
fly around him, might be warming his hands
at the fire, before the year goes out.

But the boys stacking their wood so high
don't guess that death will have to do with them.
When they start the blaze, it will go quickly:
a few hours to feast their eyes on flame,

before the white ash settles, and the man
of rags, the sacrifice, topples and dies.
My soldier once told me the world would burn
before we parted, but it was otherwise:

it burns each year, and never licks the fringe
of the dark in me, growing like the fir
that is always black out; that does not change
for autumn's light, nor the white sky of winter.

Allegiance

The skill is leaching from his hands, moment
by moment, like light through the loose weft
of an afternoon. The burnish of talent
and success, the bronze that sun left
on his taut skin is dulling, as if it were
winter with him, but it is not winter.

He is glad now of small success,
where once the best would leave him hungry.
It looked easy, but it never was:
even with skill, the shots don't come easy.
They have not come now for a long time,
and it is growing harder to see in him

what once was: is, on the odd occasion
when the grace strays across him like sunlight
over an autumn garden. But what's gone
is gone; these late rays can't kindle it.
Goodbye the fun, goodbye the fearlessness
and the endearing certainty of success

that comes of being young, and no intimate
of failure: they're on better terms now.
He has so much practice in defeat,
its gracious words, its gestures: few know how
to manage it as well. A master
of defeat, a specialist in failure.

And I would give brighter prospects a miss
to walk in the bleached leafless garden
with its sudden gleam of berries, its trees,
black and arched, its late roses half-open,
brittle with frost. There is enough to see:
what I remember here will do for me.

The Mermaid At The Sponsors' Party

We were there by courtesy of the bad baron,
the tobacco king who bankrolled the snooker,
and we edged round his sculpted feast, like folk
who should have come in at the tradesmen's door,

eyeing sticky-lacquered marrons glacés,
thinking of conkers when the husks open,
the living gleam that soon shrivels up
in a boy's pocket. We saw birds of ice,

translucent salmon roses, a chessboard chequered
in caviare and Stilton. And the mermaid,
the shining scales and rich curves of her,
carved from a smooth slab, a pale-gold rock

of butter. No intricacy was lacking
about her: she was Star-of-the-Sea Helen
to each spun-gold hair; a pretty fancy, all
of one man's time and skill for a week.

After the match, someone brought the young players,
hands in pockets: they were just boys, joking in whispers
through a dull speech; looking innocent, nibbling crisps,
hardly glancing the golden lady's way.

The Silver Kite

Coming back from Kwik-Save, kicking litter down the street
where the crazy woman in her dandelion garden
curses all comers in a monotone, he sees
the silver kite. The sky is flat blue, the glint
so high, he takes it for a jet, but it flutters
and swoops, no bigger than a scrap of tinfoil, sunlight
flashing morse off it. His mind takes off; streams out
on the wind. He misses his turning, neck cricked,
following. It dances ahead, teasing him through
that grid of shabby terraces; one with caged saplings,
vandalised already; one with black bin-bags out front,
one like another. A man could lose himself
in sameness. He rubs his neck, eyes fixed on the glitter
in the air... There was a woman once, who passed him
with an echo of scent, and he tracked the bright wake
of her hair across town, to where he'd never been.
There are familiar routes: a man's mind is printed
like a rat's in a maze: the roads that lead to work,
to the hypermarket, to the petrol station.
He is starting to feel lost; he aches with looking.
It will hurt to turn his back, to let it go,
but he is such a man. There will be something wrong
with the job in the advert, the daydreamed adventure;
the girl with her kindling hair will turn on him
a plain face, and if he should find the silver kite,
it would be brash, tawdry. So he tells himself
as he walks away, his back to the light, denying
with every step the lift, the difference in the heart.

Man Of Iron

The old man flicks a pollen speck
precisely from his shoulder.
So straight and tall he holds his back,
he might have been a soldier.

He walks the park, alone always,
inspecting the bright buttons
of upright polyanthas,
the tulip ranks, the batons

of hyacinth. It feels right
to see beauty obeying
such discipline: it kills all doubt
and justifies his being.

But when he sees the drifts of squill,
the self-sown, blue disorder,
his gaze is troubled; his eyes full
of half-remembered ardour.

He looks, then, like a man of iron
with a core of quicksilver,
a man whose dreams run riot, a man
who should have been a sailor.

Like An Old Racehorse

after Ibykos

Oh God, *again?* Dark eyelids
and a single glance,
and once more I trot up,
go through love's paces,

shivering under the saddle
like an old racehorse.
Oh God, oh no, I can't
go round again.

TRANSLATIONS

FRANCIS JAMMES 1868-1938

Clara d' Ellébeuse

I love, in the past, Clara d'Ellébeuse,
who went to a Young Ladies' Academy
and spent warm evenings under the may-trees,
reading the magazines of days gone by.

I love no other, and I feel blue rays
of light fall on my heart from her white breast.
Where is she? Where was then that happiness?
Into her room's bright clearing, branches thrust.

It may be that she isn't yet dead,
or maybe that's what we both were.
There were dead leaves on the great courtyard
in the cold wind which closed that sort of summer.

Remember where the tall vase used to stand,
with peacock's feathers, near the fancy shells?
We'd hear the grown-ups talk of lost vessels;
they'd say: *the Sandbank*, meaning Newfoundland.

Do come, my dear Clara d'Ellébeuse,
and if you still live, let us love again.
Tulips are ageing in the old garden,
come with no clothes on, Clara d'Ellébeuse.

LUDWIG HEINRICH CHRISTOPH HÖLTY 1748-76

Apoll und Dafne - Apollo & Daphne

Apollo, who was always leering
some woman's way,
(as poets will), saw in a clearing
where Daphne lay.

He tiptoed up, moaning and cooing
with lechery.
The girl decided to be going
immediately.

She fled; he followed, passion surging
and fit to choke,
until at last he'd trapped the virgin
down by a brook.

She cries: "Immortals, save my honour,"
the silly cow.
Zeus nods, and laurel leaves upon her
open and grow.

Those dainty feet, once fair as Sheba's,
are rooting fast.
And here, arse over tip, comes Phoebus,
exclaiming: "Blast!"

He leans his cheek, all wet with sobbing,
to the young wood
for which, so lately, he was throbbing,
his ex-adored.

He plucks, after a few brief whimpers,
a laurel crown
for his blond hair, next time Olympus
has a dance on.

Poor girl! Every Tom, Dick or Harry
now does the same
when feeling brave or drunk or merry.
It's a damn shame.

Soldiers and poets warring, whoring,
crowned with your locks,
like tempests through the forests roaring!
Even the cooks

are at it: you'll turn up at a wedding,
virgin-that-was;
your leaves do very well for shredding
in festive sauce.

Dear girls, you're made for love: please know it,
you'll soon grow older,
and never give a rutting poet
the old cold shoulder.

CHRISTIAN HOFMANN VON HOFMANNSWALDAU 1617-1679

Abriss Eines Verliebten - Sketch of a Man in Love

He is a sick man with an hourly fever,
a hunter who must chase his deer for ever,
a weathercock that points the same way still,
a ship headed for port in Cypris' isle,
a burning martyr, mocked by friend and foe,
a Morpheus who dreams the whole day through,
a wretched convict, clinging to his chain,
who loves the hand that measures out his pain.
He is an Aetna, fire-filled, coursing heat,
a starving man whose taste is for raw meat,
Sebastian, the mark for Eros' arrow,
Adam's true son, whom Eve poisoned with sorrow.
Business may go hang: he's a child once more,
treasuring up a ribbon, a stray hair.
Now he builds castles; now he tears them down:
one day he'll tell you man was made to mourn,
next day his heart is high; the heart that's made
of iron, following its magnet's lead.
Heaven in her face; his whole world in her lap,
his joy moors here, and this poor whitened shape
of clay is more to him than paradise:
no love, no beauty lives, but in her eyes.
(Small wonder some folk speak so ill of woman,
who brought a judgement down on being human.)
He feeds on kisses, and the salt tears slake
his thirst; with sighs and groans he kills time's ache,
and if in dreams he holds her in his arms,
she turns to air and smoke when morning comes,
for all are kin: the dream, the smoke, the lover.
He needs no call to tell him night is over;
he keeps his own alarm within his breast,
that stirs his pain and wakes him from his rest
better than he could wish. All night he lies

on thorns, and wakes with conflict in his eyes
to cry again. He never knows his mind:
he wants to die, to go to the world's end,
but his own home's the only place he is,
knowing what he would do, if he were wise,
knowing he won't; knowing he cannot fight
the hold they have on him: lust and black night.
And so he wanders strange roads without peace,
a sick mind wasting in a healthy face,
longing for darkness in the light of day,
this starless ship that cannot make its way.
It is a common sorrow, too well-known
to all, and I have sketched it as I can.
Draw back the curtain then, and let's be brief:
a portrait of the artist, done from life.

CHRISTIAN HOFMANN VON HOFMANNSWALDAU

Grabschrift einer Lustigen Jungfrawen - Epitaph of a good-time girl

The girl who lies here never wished to have
some lonely tomb: she shares a common grave,
and asked her friends to carve upon this stone:
"Dead or alive, I will not lie alone."

GEORG RUDOLF WECKHERLIN 1584-1653

An Meine Dochter, Fr. Elisabeth Trumball-
To My Daughter, Mrs. Elisabeth Trumball

Of course, you were so beautiful
and bright, I always knew you'd be
a star — why, you could read as well
as any scholar, when you were three.

I have the devil's job to master
new languages; you speak them all
just like your own. No-one learns faster;
your memory's phenomenal.

Graced with such manners and such class,
so diligent, so good, so chaste,
a pattern and a shining glass:
the field comes nowhere; you're the best.

And so I pray that all the pleasure
you gave your parents may return
to you, in just as generous measure,
when you have children of your own.

GEORG RUDOLF WECKHERLIN

Über Den Frühen Tod Fraüleins Anna Augusta Markgräfin Zu Baden
On the early death of Anna Augusta, Margravine of Baden

Your life, whose loss so brings us down,
was like a brief and pleasant day,
a star that morning scares away,
or the dawn's rose, faded so soon,
the sigh that comes from a heart moved,
a lover's anger with the loved,
a mist dissolving in the sun.

The dust stirring upon the breeze,
the dew that brings the summer in,
a snow that melts to a spring rain,
a pleasant scent that softly plays,
a flower, withered before night,
a rainbow, shimmering and bright,
a little twig each wind sways.

A shower in July, soon gone,
or ice under the sun's glare,
a glass as fragile as it's clear,
a stormy night, quiet by dawn,
a shaft of lightning flashing by,
a ray of sun splitting the sky,
or laughter, choked off in a moan.

The brief sound of a tuneful voice,
that sound's echo, fading away,
a little time, beguiled with play,
a dream that dies when sleep goes,
the swift joy of a raptor's flight,
a shadow in the noonday light,
a coil of smoke the wind undoes.

Even so your life, so briefly lent,
what was it but a day gone by,
a star, a mist, a dawn, a sigh?
Oh dust, brief anger, dew, snow, scent,
how like to ice, glass, lightning, shower,
sun, rainbow, laughter, echo, flower,
time, dream, flight, shadow, smoke, you went.

CAROLUS MALAPERTIUS

Suffering Christ

(being my 1989 English version of Simon Dach's 1651 German translation from the Latin of Carolus Malapertius of Antwerp, 1616.)

It's love that sent me spinning
to earth from the high stars.
It's why my blood is draining;
it marked me with these scars.

It is my heart's affliction,
a fever none can ease.
Not pain, nor crucifixion,
can put out flames like these.

The thorny crown that gashed me,
I took from love's own hand.
Love is the whip that lashed me,
the scorn in which I stand.

Love is this wine, sour-tasting
in all my thirst: the spear
inside my body twisting
comes as love's messenger.

What else could make me calmly
suffer the nails that drove
through hand and foot so firmly?
I owe it all to love.

And if such faith, such torment,
can earn your thanks, oh man:
why, love me, for the payment
I sought was love alone.

PAUL FLEMING 1609-1640

Grabschrift

(Epitaph, made by Herr Dr Paul Fleming for himself in Hamburg, three days before his death from pneumonia at the age of 31)

Rich in birth, goods and art, the favoured son
of luck, I was of decent parentage,
free, my own man. I could earn a fair wage,
and no-one sang like me, as was well known.
I was well-travelled; didn't get cast down
by trouble; young, carefree, alive. The age
to come will know me: I am their heritage,
thanks to the Muse, till time itself is gone.
God, father, friends, my love: if I've hurt you,
please pardon me. I want to say goodnight.
I've seen to everything, and it's all right.
Whatever Death, my enemy, can do
to me, he may: it's no great tragedy.
My life is the least living part of me.

Acknowledgements

Some of these poems and translations have appeared
in *New Welsh Review, Planet, Poetry Wales, Fine Madness* (Seattle),
BABEL (Munich), and *Can you hear?; Poems for Oxfam*, Pan Macmillan.